GOOD HOUSEKEEPING

KIDS' COOK BOOK

GOOD HOUSEKEEPING

KIDS' COOK BOOK

A FIRST STEP-BY-STEP BOOK FOR YOUNG COOKS

JANET SMITH

EBURY PRESS

PUBLISHED IN ASSOCIATION WITH

First published 1993

5 7 9 10 8 6

First published in the United Kingdom in 1993 by
EBURY PRESS
Random House, 20 Vauxhall Bridge Road, London SW1V 2SA

Random House Australia (Pty) Limited
20 Alfred Street, Milsons Point, Sydney
New South Wales 2061, Australia

Random House New Zealand Limited
18 Poland Road, Glenfield, Auckland 10, New Zealand

Random House South Africa (Pty) limited
PO Box 337, Bergvlei, South Africa

Random House UK Limited Reg. No. 954009

A CIP catalogue record for this book is available from the British Library

ISBN: 0 09 178072 1

Editor: HELEN SOUTHALL
Photographers: GUS FILGATE and KARL ADAMSON
Designer: TERRY JEAVONS

Typeset in Chichester, England
Printed and bound in Italy by New Interlitho S.p.a., Milan

Papers used by Ebury Press are natural recyclable products made from
wood grown in sustainable forests

Contents

Introduction

ooking is fun. I certainly enjoyed testing the recipes for this book, as did my enthusiastic young helpers, Elliot and Jack. These recipes are not meant to be complete meals, nor are they all necessarily the sort of things you should be eating every day; they are simply a collection of ideas for fun things to cook on rainy days, or when friends are coming to tea, or when you feel like doing something different. Whether you eat the things you cook for lunch or tea, save them for your lunchbox, or simply wolf them down as soon as they are ready, is up to you.

I hope these recipes will appeal to you, whatever your age and cooking experience. If you haven't cooked much before, you should enjoy learning about mashing, mixing and chopping; if you've already done some cooking, I hope this book will give you some new ideas. If you're not mad about cooking, but interested in art, you will enjoy decorating the biscuits and cakes in your own style – the Jewel Biscuits on page 40 make great pendants or Christmas tree decorations.

JANET SMITH

Food and Your Health

It's important to develop good eating habits right from an early age. All of us need a constant supply of vitamins and minerals, as well as carbohydrates and protein, to function properly. When you're young, it's even more important because your body is still growing and developing. The best way to ensure that you get all of these nutrients is by eating a varied diet, so aim to eat as many different kinds of foods as you can. Eat fresh fruit and vegetables every day and drink milk, or fruit juice mixed with fizzy water, rather than canned drinks. Don't snack on crisps and sweets between meals so that you're not hungry when your meals are ready. If you find that you do get hungry between meals, have a yogurt, a glass of milk or a piece of fruit. And remember that it's very important to brush your teeth really well after any snack, not just after your main meals.

Healthy food isn't boring and you probably eat lots of it already.

Things like beans or poached egg on wholemeal toast (no need to put butter on the toast); grilled fish fingers with peas and mashed potatoes; corn on the cob; grilled homemade hamburgers (see recipe on page 32) with salad; baked potatoes; cauliflower cheese; pasta with tuna or tomato sauce; and of course yogurt and fromage frais with fresh fruit like bananas, strawberries or nectarines, are all familiar healthy foods. It's important to remember that things like crisps, chips, chocolate and sweets contain hardly any nutrients and most don't contain any at all, although we eat them because they taste good. There's nothing wrong with that, providing you eat them in moderation and that you eat other things too.

Of course, if you've made a batch of biscuits or a cake, you are going to want to eat them, but instead of picking at them as soon as they are cooked, why not save them for tea or invite some friends round to share them with you.

Safety in the Kitchen

1. Always get an adult to help you, or at least make sure there is an adult nearby to help if you need it. You must ALWAYS have an adult with you when you are using knives, handling anything hot or using the food processor.

2. Wash and dry your hands before you start, and after preparing raw meat or fish.

3. Be very careful when using sharp knives and scissors. Always keep your fingers well out of the way and concentrate on what you are doing. Always use a chopping board. Don't play with knives or scissors, and keep them well out of the reach of little brothers and sisters.

4. Be very careful when using the food processor. The blades are very sharp and you must keep your fingers well away from them.

5. Never use the same chopping board for preparing raw meat or fish and cooked things, or things like salad ingredients which are going to be eaten raw.

6. Remember that the heat from the oven, grill or hob can burn. Be very careful and always wear oven gloves when putting food into or taking food out of the oven or from under the grill.

7. Don't put hot pans or baking tins on to anything that will scorch, like a polished table, or anything that will

crack, like a tiled work surface. It's a good idea to put a chopping board or heatproof mat on the work surface next to the oven so that you can put hot pans, tins or dishes straight on to it when you take them out of the oven. Don't leave hot things where someone else might touch them.

8. Steam can burn as badly as direct heat, so be very careful when draining things like cooked vegetables, rice and pasta. Never carry a pan of steaming liquid across the kitchen.

9. Hot sugar mixtures and hot oil can also burn, so be extra careful when using these ingredients.

10. Don't forget to turn off the oven, grill or hob when you have finished cooking.

11. Always wash the dishes and tidy up after cooking, not forgetting to wipe clean the work surface.

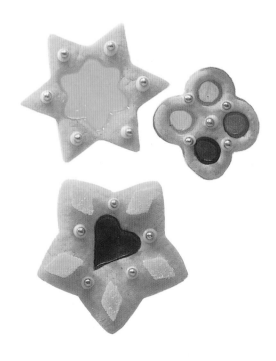

Microwave Safety

The cooking times given in the recipes are based on a 650-watt microwave oven.

1. Remember that microwave ovens, and bowls used in them, sometimes get hot after cooking. Always wear oven gloves when taking bowls out of the oven.

2. Be careful when you set the cooking time. Overcooked sugary mixtures can easily burn.

3. Don't forget to stir or turn the food occasionally during the cooking time.

4. It is very important to remember that when cooking with a microwave oven, you must never leave it unattended.

Cookery Notes

1. Get all the equipment and ingredients ready before you start.

2. Use either grams or ounces for weighing the ingredients for a recipe, not a mixture of the two.

3. When measurements are given in tablespoons or mls, use proper measuring spoons. All spoonfuls should be levelled off with a knife.

4. Use size 2 eggs unless it says otherwise in a recipe.

5. Each recipe gives an idea of how much it makes, but for some things, like biscuits for instance, this will depend on how thinly you roll out the dough and the size of the cutters you use. We used some cutters the size of small saucers, or even bigger (see the giant gingerbread man on page 51), as well as some tiny cutters no bigger than large buttons. It really is up to you whether you want to make just a few large biscuits or lots of tiny ones. For things like the Mackerel Pâté (see page 28) and the Chickpea Dip (see page 26), it is impossible to say exactly how many people they will serve, as it depends on your age and how hungry you are! The numbers of servings given on the recipes are therefore only a rough guide.

6. Each recipe includes a list of the equipment you will need to make it. These lists don't include basic things, like scales, measuring spoons and cheese graters which everybody has in their kitchen anyway.

Quick Recipes

All of the recipes in this book are fairly quick to make – but some are super-quick. So if you're really short of time, or if you are cooking with a younger brother, sister or friend who can't concentrate for very long, try one of the following; Cheese and Garlic Bread (page 22), Parmesan and Tomato Twists (page 14), Hamburgers (page 32), Mackerel Pâté (page 28), Chocolate Krispies (page 52), Fairy Cakes (page 38), Chocolate and Peanut Fudge (page 54) or Fruit Salad (page 60).

Shortcrust Pastry

MAKES 225 G
(8 OZ) PASTRY

2 Using the tips of your fingers and your thumbs, pick up a little of the flour and a couple of pieces of butter or margarine and rub them together to make the pieces of butter or margarine even smaller. As you do this, let the mixture fall back into the bowl. Keep going until all the big lumps of fat have gone and the mixture looks a bit like breadcrumbs. (This technique is called 'rubbing in'.)

1 Put the flour and salt in a bowl. Cut the butter or margarine into small cubes and drop them into the flour and salt mixture.

3 Sprinkle the water over the mixture and mix it in with a round-bladed knife until everything begins to stick together and you can shape it into a ball of dough with your hand. If it won't stick together, add a little more water, but don't add too much or the dough will become sticky. If you make a mistake and add too much water so the dough sticks to your fingers, sprinkle it with a little extra flour.

4 Sprinkle the work surface and a rolling pin with flour. Put the pastry on the work surface and roll it out with the rolling pin until it is as thin as you want it. Keep turning the pastry round as you roll it so that it is an even thickness all over. Use pastry cutters or a knife to cut the pastry to the shape and size you need.

VARIATIONS
Wholemeal Pastry Use plain wholemeal flour instead of white flour and make the pastry in the same way.
Cheese Pastry Mix 50 g (2 oz) grated Cheddar cheese into the mixture at the end of step 2, then continue to make the pastry in the same way.

Tuna Turnovers

MAKES ABOUT 24

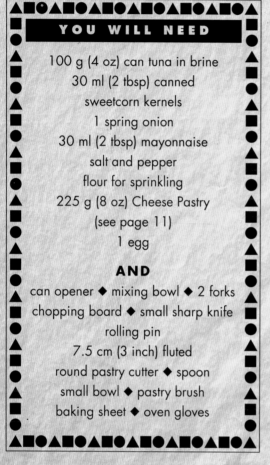

YOU WILL NEED

100 g (4 oz) can tuna in brine
30 ml (2 tbsp) canned
sweetcorn kernels
1 spring onion
30 ml (2 tbsp) mayonnaise
salt and pepper
flour for sprinkling
225 g (8 oz) Cheese Pastry
(see page 11)
1 egg

AND

can opener ◆ mixing bowl ◆ 2 forks
chopping board ◆ small sharp knife
rolling pin
7.5 cm (3 inch) fluted
round pastry cutter ◆ spoon
small bowl ◆ pastry brush
baking sheet ◆ oven gloves

Before you start, turn the oven on and set it at 200°C (400°F) mark 6.

1 Open the can of tuna and drain off the brine (which you don't need). Put the tuna in a bowl and mash it with a fork, then add the sweetcorn.

2 Put the spring onion on a chopping board and trim off the root end. Cut off the ends of the green tops. Cut the onion into small pieces and add it to the tuna mixture with the mayonnaise and a little salt and pepper. Mix with a fork or spoon until everything is well mixed.

3 Sprinkle the work surface and a rolling pin with a little flour and roll out the pastry until it is very thin. Use a 7.5 cm (3 inch) fluted round pastry cutter to cut out circles from the pastry. Re-roll the trimmings and cut out more circles until you have about 24. Spoon a little of the filling (not too much or it will leak out when it cooks) into the middle of each circle.

5 Transfer the turnovers to a baking sheet and bake in the oven for about 20 minutes or until they are golden brown. Wearing oven gloves, remove the turnovers from the oven and eat straight away, or leave to cool and eat cold.

4 Break the egg into a small bowl and whisk with a fork until the yolk and the white are mixed together. Using a pastry brush, brush a little egg around the edge of each pastry circle. Fold the pastry circles in half over the filling and press the edges together. Cut out small shapes from any leftover pastry trimmings and place on top of the turnovers as decoration. Brush all over with more beaten egg.

Tomato and Parmesan Twists

MAKES ABOUT 25

YOU WILL NEED

flour for sprinkling
450 g (1 lb) puff pastry, thawed if frozen
tomato purée
grated Parmesan cheese

AND

rolling pin ◆ knife
baking sheet ◆ oven gloves
wire cooling rack

Before you start, turn the oven on and set it at 220°C (425°F) mark 7.

2 Spread one piece of pastry with a thin layer of tomato purée and sprinkle with Parmesan cheese. Put the other piece of pastry on top of the cheese and tomato to make a pastry 'sandwich'.

1 Sprinkle the work surface and a rolling pin with a little flour and roll out the pastry until it is very thin. Trim the piece of pastry to a neat shape, if necessary, and cut it in half.

3 Cut the pastry 'sandwich' crossways into strips. Pick up one strip and twist it round a couple of times. Put it on a baking sheet and press the ends down so that they stick to the baking sheet (to stop the twists unwinding as they cook). Do the same with all the other pastry strips, then bake in the oven for about 10 minutes or until golden brown. Wearing oven gloves, remove the baking sheet from the oven and put the pastry twists on a wire rack to cool.

Vegetable Samosas

MAKES ABOUT 15

```
▲■●○▲■●○▲■●○▲■●○▲
■  YOU WILL NEED   ■
●                  ●
▲   1 medium potato ▲
■   salt and pepper ■
●  50 g (2 oz) frozen mixed vegetables ●
▲  2.5 ml (1/2 tsp) mild curry paste ▲
●  30 ml (2 tbsp) full fat soft cheese ●
▲  about 5 large sheets of filo pastry, ▲
■     thawed if frozen ■
●   vegetable oil for brushing ●
▲       poppy seeds ▲
■                  ■
●       AND        ●
▲  potato peeler ◆ sharp knife ▲
■    chopping board ■
●    small saucepan ●
▲    fork ◆ colander ▲
■  mixing bowl ◆ spoon ◆ teaspoon ■
●   baking sheet ◆ pastry brush ●
▲       oven gloves ▲
▲■●○▲■●○▲■●○▲■●○▲
```

Before you start, turn the oven on and set it at 190°C (375°F) mark 5.

1 Peel the potato, then cut it into small cubes and put it in a small saucepan. Add a pinch of salt and just enough water to cover the potato. Put the pan on the hob, bring to the boil and cook for about 10 minutes or until the potato feels soft if you spear a piece with a fork. Add the frozen vegetables and cook for 2 minutes more.

2 Put a colander in the sink and tip the vegetables into it. Allow the water to drain away, then put the vegetables in a mixing bowl. Add the curry paste, cheese and a little salt and pepper, and mix well together with a spoon. Leave to cool.

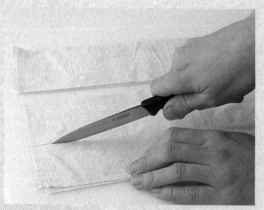

3 Lay the filo pastry sheets one on top of the other on a chopping board and cut the pastry lengthways into strips about 7.5 cm (3 inches) wide.

4 Put a teaspoon of the filling at the end of one of the strips. Fold the pastry diagonally across the filling so that it makes a triangle. Keep folding along the length of the pastry. Repeat with all the pastry and the filling to make about 15 samosas.

5 Put the samosas on a baking sheet, brush with a little oil and sprinkle with poppy seeds. Bake in the oven for about 15-20 minutes or until golden brown. Wearing oven gloves, remove the baking sheet from the oven. Eat the samosas warm, or leave to cool and eat cold.

Cheese Scones

MAKES 10-12

Before you start, turn the oven on and set it at 220°C (425°F) mark 7. Brush a baking sheet with vegetable oil.

1 Put the flour, salt, baking powder and mustard powder in a mixing bowl and mix together with a spoon. Cut the butter or margarine into small pieces and add it to the flour mixture. Using the tips of your fingers and your thumbs, pick up a little of the flour and a couple of pieces of fat and rub them together to make the pieces of fat even smaller. As you do this, let the mixture fall back into the bowl. Keep going until all the lumps have gone and the mixture looks like breadcrumbs.

2 Add most of the cheese and mix it in. Gradually add most of the milk, stirring in just enough to make the mixture stick together in a ball. If it seems dry, add the rest of the milk.

3 Sprinkle the work surface and a rolling pin with flour. Put the dough on the surface and roll it out with the rolling pin until it is about as thick as the fattest part of your hand. Cut out rounds using a 5 cm (2 inch) round pastry cutter. Gather the trimmings together into a ball, then re-roll them and cut out more rounds.

VARIATION
Cheese and Chive Scones Using kitchen scissors, snip a few chives into small pieces and add them to the flour mixture with the cheese in step 2.

4 Arrange the scones on the baking sheet and sprinkle with the rest of the cheese. Bake in the oven for about 10 minutes or until the cheese has melted and the scones are golden brown. Wearing oven gloves, remove the baking sheet from the oven and put the scones on a wire rack to cool. The scones can be eaten warm or cold.

Clown Pizzas

SERVES 6

Before you start, turn the oven on and set it at 220°C (425°F) mark 7. Brush three baking sheets with oil.

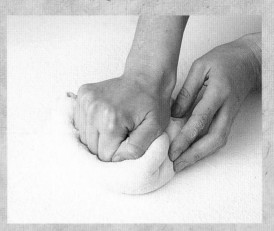

1 Make up the pizza mix following the instructions on the packet. Tip the mixture on to the work surface sprinkled with a little flour and squeeze it together with your hands to make a dough. Fold the dough over, press it down with your knuckles and turn it. Keep doing this for about 5 minutes or until your arms get very tired. This is called 'kneading'. When you've finished, the dough should feel soft and smooth.

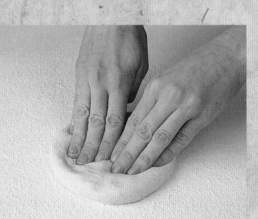

2 Cut the dough into six pieces. Sprinkle the work surface and your hands with a little flour and flatten out each piece of dough until it is about the size of a saucer. Put two circles on each baking sheet; they shouldn't touch each other.

3 Spread a little passata or pizza topping on each pizza base. Sprinkle with a little salt and pepper, then sprinkle with cheese.

4 Use the ham or salami, olives, cherry tomatoes and peppers to make clown faces on the pizzas. Bake in the oven for about 15-20 minutes or until the pizzas are well risen and golden brown. Eat hot.

Cheese and Garlic Bread

MAKES ABOUT 20 SLICES

YOU WILL NEED

125 g (4 oz) reduced-fat spread
2 garlic cloves
a small bunch of fresh chives
salt and pepper
2 small French bread sticks
or baguettes
50 g (2 oz) Cheddar or Mozzarella
cheese, grated

AND

small bowl ◆ wooden spoon
small sharp knife ◆ garlic crusher
kitchen scissors ◆ bread knife
palette knife ◆ kitchen foil
baking sheet ◆ oven gloves

Before you start, turn the oven on and set it at 180°C (350°F) mark 4.

1 Put the spread in a small bowl and stir it with a wooden spoon until it is very soft. Cut the ends off the garlic cloves and peel off the papery skins. Crush the garlic in a garlic crusher, holding the crusher over the bowl so that the crushed garlic pieces and juice fall into the spread. Using kitchen scissors, snip the chives into tiny pieces and put them in the bowl with the spread. Add a little salt and pepper, then mix everything together.

2 Using a bread knife, make deep cuts along the length of each bread stick, about 4 cm (1½ inches) apart. Cut as if you were cutting thick slices, but do not cut right through - the loaves should not fall apart.

3 Using a palette knife, spread the garlic mixture on the surfaces of the bread inside each cut.

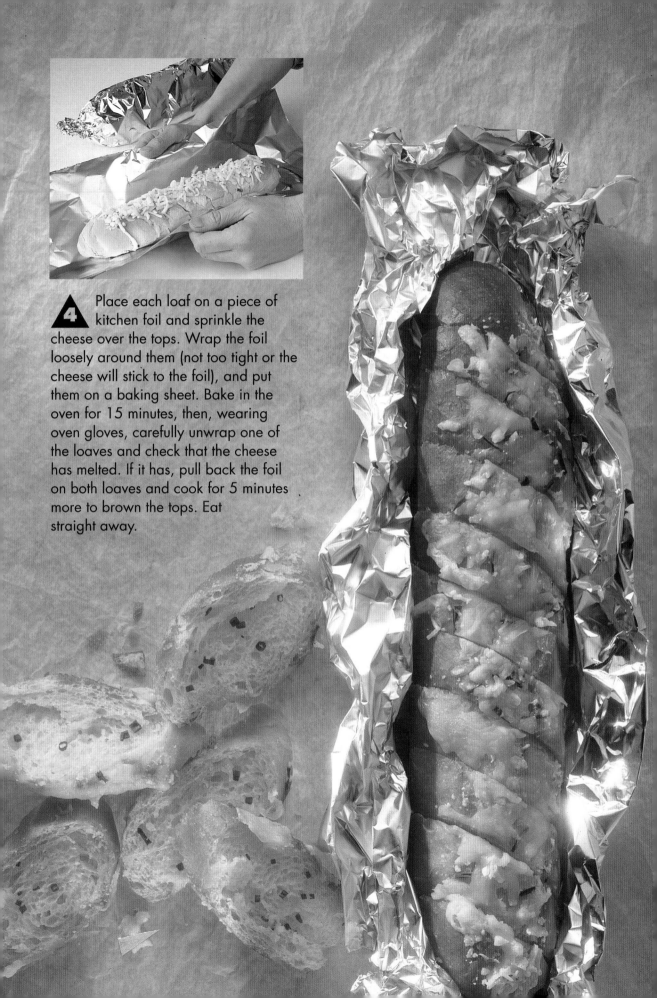

4 Place each loaf on a piece of kitchen foil and sprinkle the cheese over the tops. Wrap the foil loosely around them (not too tight or the cheese will stick to the foil), and put them on a baking sheet. Bake in the oven for 15 minutes, then, wearing oven gloves, carefully unwrap one of the loaves and check that the cheese has melted. If it has, pull back the foil on both loaves and cook for 5 minutes more to brown the tops. Eat straight away.

Egg and Cress Sandwiches

MAKES ABOUT 12

2 Put the eggs in a bowl with the mayonnaise and a little salt and pepper, and mash everything together with a fork.

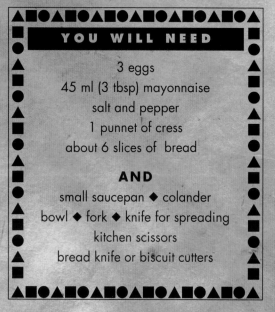

1 Put the eggs in a small saucepan and add enough cold water to cover them completely. Put the pan on the hob, bring to the boil, then lower the heat and simmer for 10 minutes. Tip the eggs out into a colander in the sink. Run cold water over the eggs for several minutes or until they feel cold. Tap the eggs on the work surface until the shells are cracked all over, then carefully peel off the shells.

3 Spread the egg mixture on three slices of bread, making sure you spread it right out to the crusts. Using kitchen scissors, snip off a little of the cress (leaving the roots still in the punnet), and sprinkle it over the egg mayonnaise. Press the remaining slices of bread on top to make sandwiches. Cut each into four with a bread knife or cut into shapes using biscuit cutters.

Chickpea Dip with Pitta Crisps

SERVES 4-6

YOU WILL NEED

400 g (14 oz) can chickpeas

30 ml (2 tbsp) light tahina (see Note)

15 ml (1 tbsp) olive oil

60 ml (4 tbsp) Greek yogurt

45 ml (3 tbsp) lemon juice

1 garlic clove ◆ salt and pepper

a pinch of mild paprika

1 black olive

about 4 large pitta breads

butter or margarine for spreading

sesame seeds for sprinkling

AND

can opener ◆ sieve ◆ mixing bowl

small sharp knife ◆ garlic crusher

potato masher ◆ spoon

serving bowl ◆ knife for spreading

chopping board ◆ baking sheet

oven gloves

Before you start, turn the oven on and set it at 200°C (400°F) mark 6.

1 Open the can of chickpeas. Hold a sieve over the sink, tip the chickpeas into it and let the liquid drain away. Run cold water over the chickpeas to rinse them, then drain again.

NOTE: Tahina is a thick paste made from ground sesame seeds and sesame oil. If you can't find it in a supermarket, try a health food shop or delicatessen.

2 Tip the chickpeas into a mixing bowl and add the tahina, oil, yogurt and lemon juice. Cut the ends off the garlic clove and peel off the papery skin. Crush the garlic in a garlic crusher, holding the crusher over the bowl so that the crushed garlic pieces and the juice drop into the mixture.

3 Using a potato masher, mash everything in the bowl together. This might be quite hard at first, but once the chickpeas have been crushed it should get easier. Keep mashing until the mixture is almost smooth. Add some salt and pepper and spoon the dip into a serving bowl. Sprinkle the paprika over the top of the dip and put the olive in the centre.

4 Split the pitta breads in half right through the middle. Spread what were the insides of the pittas with butter or margarine and sprinkle with sesame seeds. Cut the pieces into triangles and spread them out on a baking sheet. Bake in the oven for about 10 minutes or until the pitta pieces are light brown and crisp. Wearing oven gloves, carefully remove the baking sheet from the oven and serve the pitta crisps with the dip.

Mackerel Pâté

SERVES 6

2 Put the mackerel on a board. Using a fork, carefully remove the fish from the skin. Throw away the skin and break the fish into small pieces with the fork.

3 Add the fish to the cheese mixture and season with a little salt and some pepper. Mix together and spoon into a small serving bowl or spread on to fish shapes cut with biscuit cutters from pitta breads or slices of toast.

1 Put the cheese in a mixing bowl with the lemon juice and horseradish. Beat it all together with a wooden spoon until the cheese is soft and creamy.

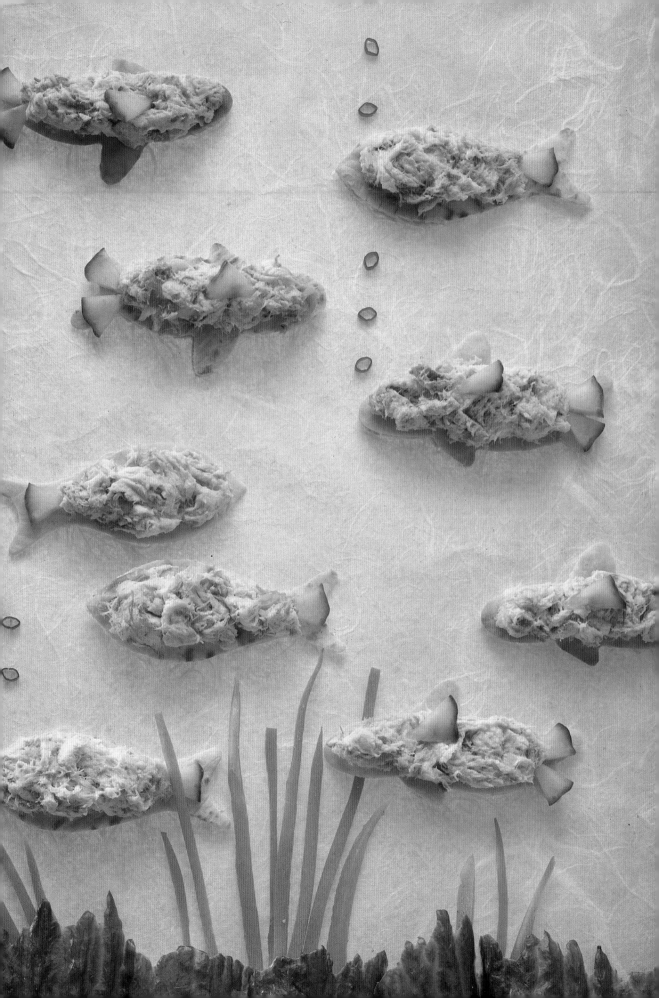

Barbecue Chicken Drumsticks

MAKES 8

YOU WILL NEED

60 ml (4 tbsp) tomato ketchup

15 ml (1 level tbsp) dark brown sugar

15 ml (1 tbsp) mild mustard

30 ml (2 tbsp) dark soy sauce

1 garlic clove (if you like it)

8 chicken drumsticks

AND

mixing bowl ◆ chopping board

small sharp knife

garlic crusher (if used)

spoon ◆ cling film (if used)

roasting tin ◆ oven gloves

If you are going to cook the chicken straight away, turn the oven on and set it at 200°C (400°F) mark 6 before you start to prepare it.

1 Put the ketchup, sugar, mustard and soy sauce in a large bowl. If you want to add the garlic, cut the ends off the garlic clove and peel off the papery skin. Crush the garlic in a garlic crusher, holding the crusher over the bowl so that the crushed garlic pieces and juice drop into the mixture. Mix together well with a spoon. Make two deep cuts in each drumstick with a sharp knife. (This lets the flavour of the sauce get right into the chicken.) Drop the drumsticks into the sauce.

2 Stir the drumsticks around so they are all covered in sauce. If you can wait, the chicken will be more tasty if you leave it to soak (marinate) in the sauce for about 30 minutes. Cover the bowl with cling film and leave it in a cool place in the kitchen. (If you can't wait, don't worry, the chicken will still taste good!) After the chicken has been marinating for about 15 minutes, turn the oven on and set it at 200°C (400°F) mark 6.

3 Tip the drumsticks and sauce into a roasting tin. Cook them in the oven for about 35 minutes or until they look very brown and crispy.

4 To check if the drumsticks are cooked, put on oven gloves and remove the roasting tin from the oven. Make a small cut in the thickest end of one of the drumsticks and see if any pink juices run out. If they do, cook the drumsticks for a bit longer and test again. When cooked, the juices that run out will not be pink. Eat hot or cold.

Hamburgers

MAKES 4

2 Divide the mixture into four and shape one portion into a burger with your hands. Repeat with the rest of the mixture to make four burgers. Try to make them all roughly the same size so that they cook evenly. To make smaller burgers, divide the mixture into eight. Put the burgers on the wire rack in a grill pan and cook under a hot grill until they are brown on one side.

1 Put the beef in a bowl and mash it with a fork to break up any large lumps. Cut the root ends off the spring onions and cut off the ends of the green tops. Cut the onions into small pieces and add them to the meat with plenty of salt and pepper. Mix everything together.

3 Wearing oven gloves, turn the burgers over with a fish slice and cook for 5 minutes more or until they are cooked right through. To check if they are cooked, make a cut in the centre of one burger and press lightly. The juices that run out should be clear. If they are pink, cook the burgers for a few minutes more. Serve straight away in sesame seed buns with salad.

VARIATION
Veggieburgers Mash 225 g (8 oz)
original tofu in a bowl, and add
125 g (4 oz) grated carrot, 125 g
(4 oz) breadcrumbs, 3 chopped
spring onions, 5 ml (1 level tsp)
mixed dried herbs, 15 ml (1 tbsp)
vegetarian Worcestershire sauce,
5 ml (1 tsp) yeast extract and 1 small
egg. Mix well, then shape into
burgers and cook in the same way as
Hamburgers for 3 minutes each side.

Baked Potato Boats

SERVES 4

YOU WILL NEED

2 baking potatoes
50 g (2 oz) full fat soft cheese
a little milk
salt and pepper
225 g (8 oz) can baked beans
4 slices of Edam cheese

AND

fork ◆ oven gloves
chopping board ◆ knife
spoon ◆ mixing bowl
potato masher ◆ can opener
baking sheet ◆ 4 cocktail sticks

Before you start, turn the oven on and set it at 200°C (400°F) mark 6.

1 Prick the potatoes all over with a fork (to stop them exploding as they cook), and bake them in the oven for about 1 hour or until they are soft. To see if the potatoes are soft, put on oven gloves and squeeze the potatoes gently. (If you are in a hurry, cook the potatoes in the microwave on HIGH for about 10 minutes instead. Take them out of the microwave and put them in the oven for 15 minutes to make the skins crisp.)

2 Still wearing oven gloves, cut the hot potatoes in half and use a spoon to scoop the filling out into a bowl, being careful not to break the potato skins. Add the soft cheese and a drop of milk to the potato and mash with a potato masher until all the lumps have gone. Add a little salt and pepper.

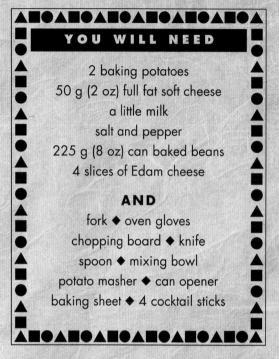

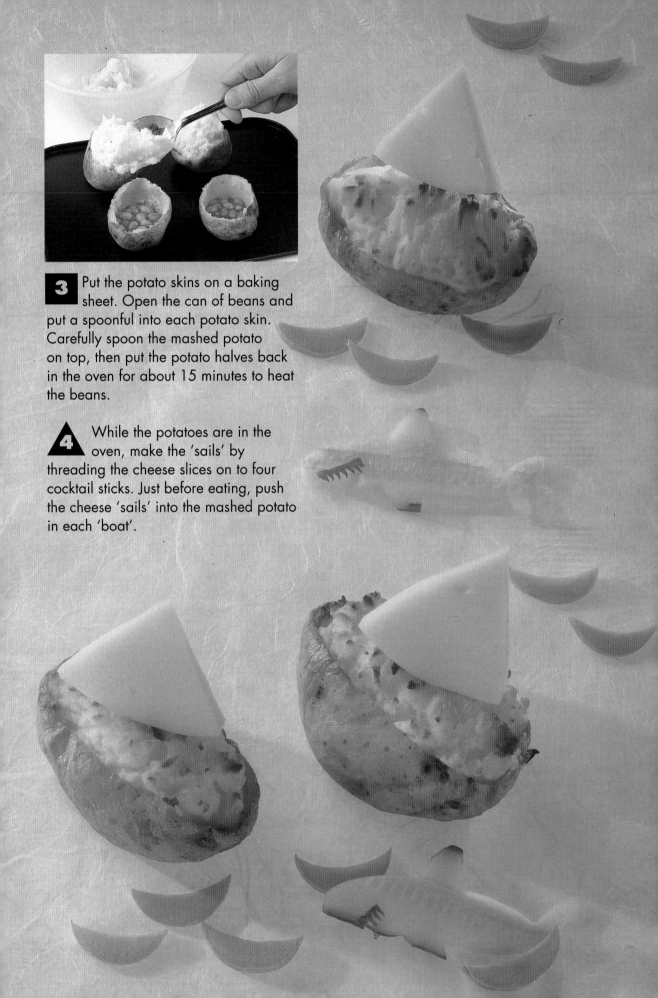

3 Put the potato skins on a baking sheet. Open the can of beans and put a spoonful into each potato skin. Carefully spoon the mashed potato on top, then put the potato halves back in the oven for about 15 minutes to heat the beans.

4 While the potatoes are in the oven, make the 'sails' by threading the cheese slices on to four cocktail sticks. Just before eating, push the cheese 'sails' into the mashed potato in each 'boat'.

Glacé Icing

MAKES ENOUGH TO DECORATE 18 FAIRY CAKES

YOU WILL NEED

225 g (8 oz) icing sugar
about 30 ml (2 tbsp) warm water

AND

sieve ◆ mixing bowl
wooden spoon

2 Pour a little of the water into the sugar and mix with a wooden spoon to make a smooth, gooey paste. If the mixture is too thick, add a little more water, but don't add too much or the icing will run off the cakes or biscuits.

1 Tip the icing sugar into a sieve and sift it into the mixing bowl. This stops the icing being lumpy.

3 To check that the icing is not too thin, dip the wooden spoon in it, lift it out with its back facing upwards and see if the icing stays on it in a thin coating. If it all runs off, it is too runny! Don't worry, just sift in a little extra icing sugar.

VARIATIONS
Coloured Icing Add a few drops of food colouring.
Chocolate Sift 15 ml (1 level tbsp) cocoa powder into the bowl with the icing sugar.
Fruit Use fruit juice (orange or lemon) instead of water.

4 Use the icing to top fairy cakes, sponge cakes, or biscuits. Decorations, such as sweets, sultanas and chocolate drops, can be stuck into the icing once it's on the cake, but make sure you put them on straight away, before the icing sets.

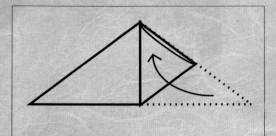

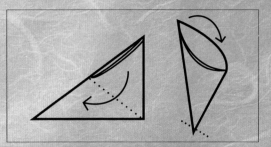

5 If you want to pipe glacé icing on to a cake, you'll need to make a piping bag. Cut a 25 cm (10 inch) square of greaseproof paper and fold it diagonally in half to make a triangle. Holding the paper with the longest side of the triangle at the bottom, fold the righthand point up to meet the top point.

7 Fold the triangle in half again. Turn this small triangle so the longest side is vertical, and open it out into a cone. Twist the top points together to hold the cone in shape.

8 Fill the bag with glacé icing and fold the top over to stop the icing spilling out. Gently squeeze the bag at the top and the icing should come out of the pointed end. If it doesn't, cut a tiny piece off the end with a pair of scissors.

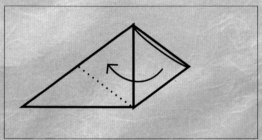

6 Fold the new righthand point over towards the middle of the opposite sloping side to make a triangle that is half the size of the original one.

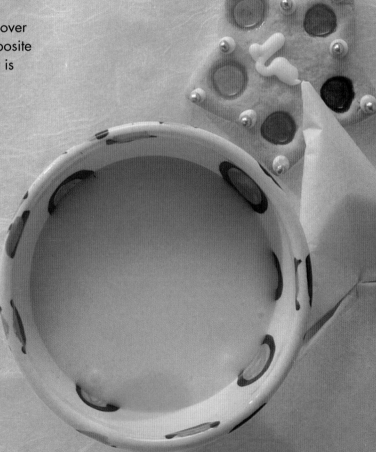

37

Fairy Cakes

MAKES ABOUT 18

YOU WILL NEED

125 g (4 oz) self-raising
white flour
2.5 ml (1/2 level tsp) baking powder
125 g (4 oz) caster sugar
125 g (4 oz) soft tub margarine
2 eggs ◆ 15 ml (1 tbsp) milk
glacé icing (see page 36)
glacé cherries or sweets

AND

paper cake cases ◆ 2 bun tins
mixing bowl ◆ wooden spoon
teaspoon ◆ oven gloves
wire cooling rack ◆ palette knife

Before you start, turn the oven on and set it at 200°C (400°F) mark 6. Put a paper case into 18 of the holes in two bun tins.

2 Put a teaspoonful of mixture into each paper case. Don't try to put too much in or it will leak out during cooking. Bake the cakes in the oven for about 10-15 minutes or until they are golden brown. Wearing oven gloves, take the cakes out of the oven and put them on a wire rack to cool.

3 When the cakes are cold, spread the tops with glacé icing and decorate with glacé cherries or sweets. Leave the icing to set before eating.

1 Put the flour, baking powder, sugar, margarine, eggs and milk in a mixing bowl and mix with a wooden spoon until the mixture is pale and very soft and you can't see any lumps of margarine.

VARIATIONS
Chocolate Fairy Cakes Replace 30 ml (2 level tbsp) of the flour with cocoa powder, and make the cakes in the same way.
Or Add 50 g (2 oz) chocolate drops, sultanas or chopped dried apricots to the mixture at the end of step 1, stir in well and continue to make the cakes in the same way.

Jewel Biscuits

MAKES ABOUT 10

YOU WILL NEED

125 g (4 oz) butter or margarine
175 g (6 oz) plain white flour
50 g (2 oz) caster sugar
a few drops of vanilla essence
flour for sprinkling
coloured boiled sweets
glacé icing (see page 36) or ready-
made piping icing
silver balls

AND

3 baking sheets
non-stick baking parchment
mixing bowl ◆ wooden spoon
rolling pin ◆ biscuit cutters
skewer ◆ oven gloves
palette knife ◆ wire cooling rack
ribbon or thread

Before you start, turn the oven on and set it at 180°C (350°F) mark 4.

1 Cover a baking sheet with a sheet of non-stick baking parchment. Do the same again with two more baking sheets. (If the paper won't stay flat, brush the baking sheets with a little oil before putting the paper on.)

2 Put the butter or margarine in a mixing bowl and stir it with a wooden spoon until it is very soft. This will be quite easy if you are using soft tub margarine, but if you are using butter from the fridge it will take quite a long time. If the butter won't soften, leave it in a warm place for a little while (or put it in the microwave on HIGH for 20 seconds), then try again.

3 Add the flour, sugar and vanilla essence to the butter or margarine and mix everything together with a wooden spoon. Keep mixing until the mixture begins to stick together in lumps, then mix it with your fingers until it sticks together like a dough. Sprinkle some flour on the work surface and a rolling pin, then roll out the dough.

4 Using biscuit cutters, cut the dough into different shapes and arrange the biscuits on the prepared baking sheets. Using small cutters, cut a shape from the middle of each biscuit and put a sweet in each hole.

6 When the biscuits are cold, decorate them with glacé icing and silver balls. Thread ribbon or thread through the small holes in the biscuits if you want to hang them up.

VARIATION
To make multicoloured jewelled centres, like in the photograph, cut a very large hole in the centre of the biscuit and fill with two or three sweets.

5 Make a small hole at the top of each biscuit with a skewer. Bake the biscuits in the oven for about 10 minutes or until the biscuits are pale golden brown and the sweets have melted. Wearing oven gloves, remove the biscuits from the oven and wiggle the skewer in the small holes again to make sure they haven't closed up. Using a palette knife, remove the biscuits from the baking sheets (be careful, the melted sweets will be very hot) and put on a wire rack to cool.

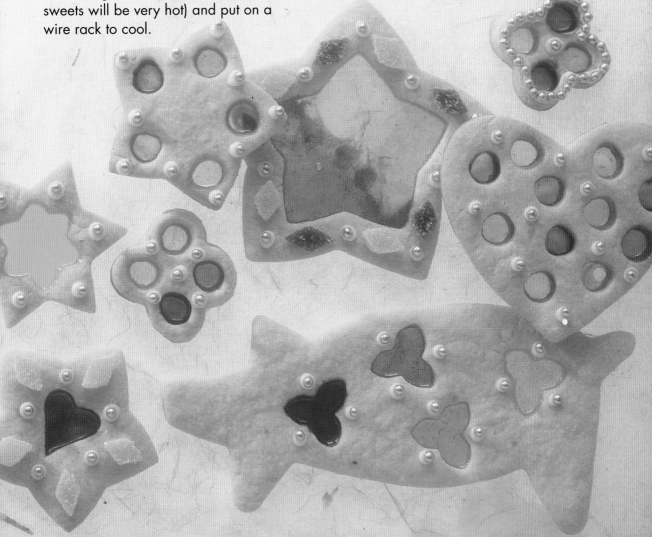

Marble Birthday Cake

SERVES 6

YOU WILL NEED

vegetable oil for brushing

125 g (4 oz) plain white flour

125 g (4 oz) self-raising white flour

5 ml (1 level tsp) baking powder

175 g (6 oz) soft tub margarine

30 ml (2 tbsp) milk

175 g (6 oz) caster sugar

5 ml (1 tsp) vanilla essence

3 eggs

pink food colouring (or any other
colour you like)

30 ml (2 level tbsp) cocoa powder

175 g (6 oz) milk or plain chocolate

AND

18 cm (7 inch) deep round
cake tin ◆ pastry brush

greaseproof paper ◆ pencil

scissors ◆ food processor

3 mixing bowls ◆ spoons

plastic spatula

round-bladed knife ◆ oven gloves

wire cooling rack

heatproof bowl ◆ saucepan

palette knife

sweets and candles

Before you start, turn the oven on and set it at 180°C (350°F) mark 4.

1 Pour a few drops of oil into the cake tin. Use a pastry brush to spread it all over the inside. Put the tin on a piece of greaseproof paper and draw round it with a pencil. Cut the circle out and press it into the bottom of the tin. Brush with a little more oil.

2 Put the flours, baking powder, margarine, 15 ml (1 tbsp) of the milk, the sugar and vanilla essence in a food processor. Crack the eggs into a small bowl, pick out any pieces of shell, then pour the egg into the flour mixture. Put the lid on the food processor and turn the machine on for just 2 minutes or until everything is mixed together. (Don't leave it running too long or the cake will not rise.)

3 Put about one third of the cake mixture in a bowl, add a few drops of food colouring and mix it in evenly with a spoon. Put another third of the mixture in another bowl and add the cocoa powder and the rest of the milk. Mix well.

6 Carefully, run a knife around the edge of the cake between the cake and the tin, then turn out the cake on to a wire rack to cool. Peel the greaseproof paper off the bottom.

4 Put a tablespoon of white cake mixture in the cake tin, then add a spoonful of chocolate mixture, followed by a spoonful of pink mixture. Keep doing this until all the cake mixtures are in the tin (use a plastic spatula to help you get all the mixture out of the food processor).

7 When the cake is cold, you can decorate it. Break the chocolate into squares and put it in a heatproof bowl. Put a little water in a saucepan and heat until it simmers. Stand the bowl over the water (the bowl should not touch the water) and turn the heat down to very low. Stir the chocolate until it has melted. (If you have a microwave oven, you can melt the chocolate on HIGH for 2 minutes.) Pour the hot chocolate over the top of the cake and spread it out with a palette knife. Decorate with sweets and candles, then leave the chocolate to set before eating.

5 Using a round-bladed knife, make the shape of an eight right through the cake mixture. This helps to mix the colours together. Level the surface of the mixture in the tin. Bake the cake in the oven for about 1 hour or until the cake is golden brown on the top. Wearing oven gloves, press the cake very gently on top. If it is cooked, it will spring back into shape.

SAFETY NOTE
Ask an adult to help you use the food processor. The blades are very sharp and you need to be extra careful not to touch them, especially when taking the cake mixture out of the processor.

Dinosaur Biscuits

MAKES ABOUT 16

YOU WILL NEED

25 g (1 oz) plain white flour
175 g (6 oz) plain wholemeal flour
5 ml (1 level tsp) baking powder
25 g (1 oz) caster sugar
25 g (1oz) rolled oats
75 g (3 oz) butter or margarine
about 75 ml (5 tbsp) milk
flour and icing sugar for rolling
450 g (1 lb) packet ready-to-roll icing
food colouring

AND

mixing bowl ◆ knife ◆ rolling pin
dinosaur biscuit cutters
2 baking sheets
oven gloves ◆ wire cooling racks
pastry brush

Before you start, turn the oven on and
set it at 200°C (400°F) mark 6.

1 Put the flours, baking powder,
sugar and oats in a mixing bowl.
Cut the butter or margarine into small
pieces and add it to the flour. Using the
tips of your fingers and your thumbs,
pick up a few pieces of butter or
margarine and some of the flour mixture
and rub them together so that the pieces
of butter or margarine get even smaller.
As you do this, let the mixture fall back
into the bowl. Keep rubbing the
ingredients together until all the big
lumps have gone and the mixture looks
a bit like breadcrumbs. (This technique
is called 'rubbing in'.)

2 Gradually add a little milk,
mixing in just enough with your
fingers to make the mixture stick
together in a ball. Add a little more milk
if the dough seems dry.

4 When the biscuits are cold, colour a little of the ready-to-roll icing green with a few drops of food colouring. Sprinkle the work surface and a rolling pin with icing sugar and roll out the icing. Use biscuit cutters to cut out dinosaur shapes the same as the biscuits. Brush the underside of the icing with a little water and stick the shapes on to the biscuits.

5 Colour the rest of the icing different colours and use to make scales, eyes and teeth as needed.

3 Sprinkle a little flour on the work surface and a rolling pin, and roll out the dough until it is very thin. Cut out dinosaur shapes using biscuit cutters. Put the biscuits on baking sheets and bake in the oven for 10-15 minutes or until pale brown. Wearing oven gloves, take the baking sheets out of the oven and carefully put the biscuits on wire racks to cool.

Gingerbread Biscuits

MAKES ABOUT 12

```
▲■●▲■●▲■●▲■●▲■●▲■●▲
■                           ■
●     YOU WILL NEED         ●
▲                           ▲
■    vegetable oil for brushing    ■
●   350 g (12 oz) plain white flour   ●
▲  5 ml (1 level tsp) bicarbonate of soda  ▲
■   10 ml (2 level tsp) ground ginger   ■
●  125 g (4 oz) butter or hard margarine  ●
▲  175 g (6 oz) light soft brown sugar   ▲
●             1 egg              ●
▲          golden syrup          ▲
■      extra flour for sprinkling    ■
●         currants or sweets       ●
▲  glacé icing (see page 36) or ready-  ▲
■        made piping icing         ■
●                                 ●
▲            AND               ▲
■  3 baking sheets ◆ pastry brush  ■
●  mixing bowl ◆ knife, fork and spoon  ●
▲     small bowl ◆ rolling pin      ▲
■  biscuit cutters (people, bears)  ■
●        wire cooling rack         ●
▲■●▲■●▲■●▲■●▲■●▲■●▲
```

Before you start, turn the oven on and set it at 190°C (375°F) mark 5.

1 Pour a tiny drop of oil on to a baking sheet, then use a pastry brush to brush it all over the surface. Do the same to two more baking sheets.

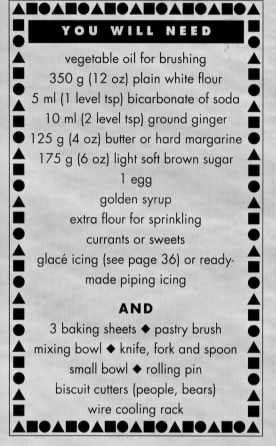

2 Put the flour, bicarbonate of soda and ginger in a mixing bowl and mix together. Cut the butter or margarine into very small cubes and add them to the flour. Using the tips of your fingers and your thumbs, pick up a little of the flour and a couple of pieces of butter or margarine, and rub them together to make the pieces of butter or margarine even smaller. As you do this, let the mixture fall back into the bowl. Keep rubbing the ingredients together until all the big lumps have gone. (This technique is called 'rubbing in'). Mix in the sugar.

3 Crack the egg open on the side of a small bowl and let all the egg run into the bowl. If any pieces of egg shell fall into the bowl, pick them out with a spoon or with a larger piece of broken shell. Hold a metal tablespoon in hot water for a couple of minutes, shake it dry, then quickly use it to spoon 60 ml (4 tbsp) syrup out of the tin and into the bowl with the egg. Because the spoon is warm, the syrup won't stick to it.

5 Cut the dough in half. Sprinkle a rolling pin with flour and roll out one half of the dough until it is very thin. Using biscuit cutters, cut out gingerbread men and women and teddy bears. Use currants or sweets to make eyes and buttons. Carefully lift the biscuits on to the oiled baking sheets. Roll out the other half of the dough and cut out more biscuits. Bake all the biscuits in the oven for 12-15 minutes or until the biscuits look a little darker in colour (don't worry if they seem soft - they will become crisp as they cool). Transfer the biscuits to a wire rack to cool completely. When the biscuits are cold, decorate them with icing and sweets.

4 Using a fork, mix the syrup and egg, then pour into the flour mixture. Mix everything together and tip it out on to the work surface sprinkled with a little flour. Squeeze everything together with your hands to make a dough.

Chocolate Krispies

MAKES ABOUT 60

2 Put the Mars bars, syrup and butter or margarine in a non-stick saucepan. Put the pan on the hob and heat *very* gently until the Mars bars have melted, stirring all the time with a wooden spoon to prevent the mixture sticking. (If you have a microwave oven, put the ingredients in a heatproof bowl and microwave on HIGH for about 2 minutes or until melted, stirring occasionally.)

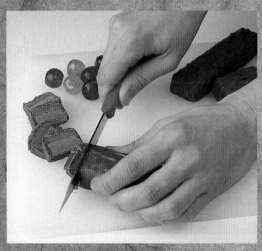

1 Slice the Mars bars and cut the cherries into very small pieces.

3 Add the cherries, raisins and Rice Krispies and mix everything together. Do this quite quickly before the Mars mixture sets. Spoon it into a non-stick tin measuring about 25 x 16 cm (10 x 6½ inches) and pat it down to level the surface. Leave to set completely.

4 Turn the tin upside-down on a board and tap it with your hand until the mixture falls out in one piece. Cut into small squares or fingers (it is *very* rich).

Chocolate and Peanut Fudge

MAKES ABOUT 60 PIECES

YOU WILL NEED

vegetable oil for brushing
225 g (8 oz) plain chocolate
50 g (2 oz) full fat soft cheese
a walnut – sized piece of butter
50 ml (2 fl oz) milk
a few drops of vanilla essence
450 g (1 lb) icing sugar
125 g (4 oz) roasted unsalted peanuts

AND

20 cm (8 inch) square ovenproof dish
or cake tin
pastry brush
greaseproof paper
pencil or pen ◆ scissors
heavy-based non-stick saucepan
wooden spoon ◆ sieve
large mixing bowl ◆ knife
airtight container

VARIATION

Replace the peanuts with your own favourite nuts or a mixture of nuts and raisins.

1 Pour a few drops of oil into a 20 cm (8 inch) square ovenproof dish or cake tin and use a pastry brush to brush it all over the inside. Put the dish or tin on a sheet of greaseproof paper and draw round it with a pencil. Cut out the square with scissors and press it into the base of the dish or tin.

2 Break the chocolate into small squares and put it in a heavy-based non-stick saucepan with the cheese, butter and milk. Turn the heat on very low and cook the mixture gently, stirring all the time with a wooden spoon, until the chocolate has melted. (If you have a microwave oven, put the ingredients in a small heatproof bowl and microwave on HIGH for about 2 minutes or until melted. Don't forget to use oven gloves as the bowl will get hot.) Add the vanilla essence.

3 Put the icing sugar in a sieve and sift it into a large mixing bowl. Pour the icing sugar into the chocolate mixture and mix everything together. Cook for 1 minute more or until the fudge mixture is smooth and thick. Mix in about half the peanuts and pour the mixture into the dish or tin. Sprinkle the rest of the peanuts on top and push them down gently so that they stick.

4 Leave the fudge in the fridge to set, then turn it out and cut it into small squares. Store the fudge in an airtight container in the fridge or it will go sticky.

Banana and Sultana Teabread

SERVES 6

```
▲■○▲■○▲■○▲■○▲■○▲■○▲■○▲
■  ┌──────────────────────┐  ■
●  │   YOU WILL NEED      │  ●
▲  └──────────────────────┘  ▲
■                            ■
●     vegetable oil for brushing     ●
▲    2 large or 3 medium ripe bananas  ▲
■      60 ml (4 tbsp) thick honey    ■
●       juice of ½ small lemon       ●
▲    125 g (4 oz) soft tub margarine   ▲
■  225 g (8 oz) self-raising white flour ■
●   5 ml (1 level tsp) baking powder  ●
▲     125 g (4 oz) caster sugar      ▲
■            2 eggs               ■
●      50 g (2 oz) sultanas        ●
▲                                ▲
■             AND                ■
●                                ●
▲    1.4 litre (2½ pint) loaf tin    ▲
■  pastry brush ◆ greaseproof paper  ■
●    pencil or pen ◆ scissors      ●
▲   mixing bowl ◆ potato masher    ▲
■   wooden spoon ◆ oven gloves    ■
●        wire cooling rack         ●
▲                                ▲
▲■○▲■○▲■○▲■○▲■○▲■○▲■○▲
```

Before you start, turn the oven on and set it at 180°C (350°F) mark 4.

1 Pour a few drops of oil into a 1.4 litre (2½ pint) loaf tin and use a pastry brush to brush it all over the inside of the tin. Cut a piece of greaseproof paper that's the same width as the base but twice the length of the tin. Press the paper down into the tin so that the ends of the paper hang over the ends of the tin.

2 Peel the bananas and break them into small pieces. Put them in a bowl with the honey and lemon juice, and mash them with a potato masher until they are very soft.

3 Add the margarine and mash it in, still using the potato masher. (Don't worry if the mixture looks horrible and lumpy.)

4 Add all of the remaining ingredients and beat everything together with a wooden spoon. Spoon the mixture into the tin and level the surface. Make a shallow hole in the middle with the spoon. Bake in the oven for about 1¼ hours or until it is dark golden brown. Wearing oven gloves, take the cake out of the oven and press it very gently on top. If it is cooked, the top will spring back up again. Leave the cake to cool in the tin for about 10 minutes, then turn it out on to a wire rack, peel off the greaseproof paper, and leave the cake to cool completely.

VARIATIONS
Replace half of the white flour with the same amount of self-raising wholemeal flour. Use chocolate drops or chips instead of sultanas.

Apple
Pastries

MAKES ABOUT 9

```
YOU WILL NEED

flour for sprinkling
450 g (1 lb) puff pastry,
thawed if frozen
about 4 Granny Smith apples
1 egg ◆ caster sugar
icing sugar

AND

rolling pin
star and heart pastry or biscuit cutters
2 baking sheets
sharp knife ◆ potato peeler
small bowl ◆ fork ◆ pastry brush
oven gloves ◆ small sieve
```

Before you start, turn the oven on and set it at 220°C (425°F) mark 7.

2 Cut the apples into quarters, peel them with a potato peeler, and cut out the cores. Cut the apples into very thick slices.

3 Break the egg into a small bowl (pick out any pieces of shell) and mix it lightly with a fork to break up the yolk. Using a pastry brush, brush the tops of the pastry shapes with a little of the beaten egg. Arrange the apple slices on top.

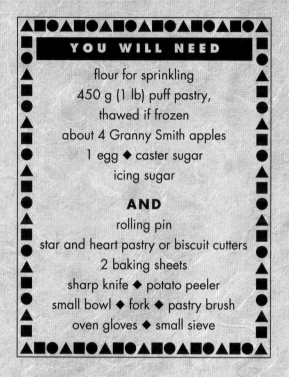

1 Sprinkle the work surface with flour and roll out the pastry until it is very thin. Cut out about nine large shapes using cutters and put them on two baking sheets.

4 Sprinkle the apples with caster sugar (use a sugar dredger if you have one) and bake in the oven for about 25 minutes or until the apples are brown and the pastry looks puffy and brown around the edges. Wearing oven gloves, take the baking sheets out of the oven and put the pastries on a large plate. Put a little icing sugar in a sieve and sift it over the tops of the apples before serving.

Fruit Salad

SERVES 6

2 Chop any large pieces of pineapple into bite-sized pieces and put all the pineapple in a mixing bowl. Wash the grapes, strawberries and apple, if using. Pull the grapes off their stalks and add them to the pineapple. Pull the stalks off the strawberries, cut any large ones in half or slices and add them to the pineapple.

1 Cut the pineapple in half lengthways, right through the fruit and the leafy top. It's easiest to do this with a large sharp knife, so ask an adult to help you. When you have cut it in half, run the knife around the inside of each half about 2.5 cm (1 inch) in from the skin. Using a metal spoon, scoop the pineapple flesh out. Cut out and discard the tough central core.

3 Peel the satsumas or clementines, break the fruit into segments and pull off as much of the white stringy pith as you can. Mix the segments with the other fruit and the fruit juice in the bowl. Peel and slice the banana and mix it in as well. Cut the apple into quarters and cut out the core. Cut the apple into neat slices and mix it into the fruit salad.

4 Spoon the fruit into the pineapple shells for serving. Don't wait too long before eating the fruit salad or the banana and apple will go brown.

VARIATION
Tropical fruit salad Prepare the pineapple in the same way but replace the other fruit with some of your favourite tropical fruits. You can choose from mango, star fruit, kiwi, melon and papaya – whatever is available in the shops. Use pineapple juice or mixed tropical fruit juice.

Raspberry Yogurt Ice

SERVES 8-10

YOU WILL NEED

450 g (1 lb) fresh raspberries

105 ml (7 tbsp) icing sugar

30 ml (2 tbsp) golden syrup

150 ml (5 fl oz) raspberry yogurt (not low fat)

300 ml (1/2 pint) thick double cream

2 very fresh egg whites

AND

sieve ◆ 3 mixing bowls

wooden spoon ◆ balloon whisk

large metal spoon

shallow plastic freezer

container (with lid)

Before you start, ask someone to switch the freezer to 'fast freeze'.

2 Put the cream in a bowl. Using a balloon whisk, stir the cream round and round very quickly until it gets a bit thicker. Stir it into the raspberry mixture. Wash and dry the whisk.

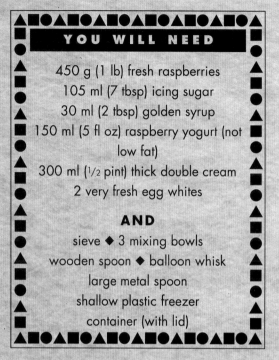

1 Put the raspberries in a sieve over a mixing bowl and push the raspberries through the sieve using a wooden spoon. (Throw away the raspberry pips.) Mix half of the sugar and the syrup into the raspberry mush in the bowl, then stir until it has dissolved. Stir in the yogurt.

3 Put the egg whites in another clean bowl with the rest of the sugar. Using the clean whisk, whisk the egg white round and round until it becomes stiff and white. This will take quite a while and will make your arm ache, but keep going. When the mixture is ready, you should be able to turn the bowl upside-down without the egg white falling out!

4 Using a large metal spoon, carefully mix the egg white into the raspberry mixture, making sure that you mix it in evenly and lightly. Pour the mixture into a shallow plastic freezer container, cover with a lid and freeze for about 4 hours or until firm. When it is firm, transfer it to the fridge and leave it there for 10 minutes before trying to spoon it into bowls to eat. Eat on the day of or day after making.
(Don't forget to ask someone to turn the freezer back to 'normal'.)

VARIATIONS
Strawberry Yogurt Ice Use ripe strawberries instead of raspberries and use strawberry yogurt. Slice the strawberries and mash them with a potato masher before pushing them through the sieve.
Yogurt and Marshmallow Ice Mix two handfuls of baby marshmallows into the fruit mixture (strawberry or raspberry) with the whisked egg white.

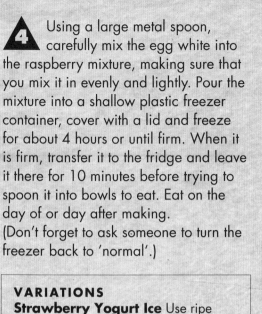

Index